for Your Dog

By Sally Montrucchio
Next Step Service Dogs
Training Director
nextstepservicedogs.org

Acknowledgments

A hearty thanks to all the service dog trainers and clients who have challenged me to find creative ways to train over the years. The journey has been a lot of fun and very rewarding.

A special thanks to all who have helped me create this games toolbox, especially Kadyn Victorino, age 8.

A very special thanks to my grandsons, Kaiya and Kanoa Montrucchio, and my nephew, Harrison Mc Creery, who continue to teach me how to play.

This games book will always be in progress.

Sally Montrucchio
Service Dog Training Director
Next Step Service Dogs

How to Use This Games Book

This is an activity, exercise and game book

~ to make your dog training more interesting and
   fun.
~ that you can adjust to your training needs.
~ to inspire you to create new activities, exercises
   or games.

Use a clicker or another marker to be most effective.

Table of Contents
(Games in alphabetical order)

Cue Exercise cont.

Distraction

Greeting

Persistence

Problem-Solving

Recall

Retrieval

Rewards

Scent Discrimination

Self-Control

Your Training Notes

Bags
Paper & Plastic

All levels

Purpose: challenge, problem-solving, retrieval

What you will need: different sized paper and plastic bags, retrieval items to put into the bags

Instructions:
1. Use positive reinforcement.
2. Start by placing a toy in a bag.
3. Hold the bag open so the dog can retrieve it.
4. Graduate to non-toys.
5. Then place the bag on the ground so the dog has a harder time fetching the item out of the bag.
6. If the dog rips the bag, reset the dog by putting him in a sit and start over.
7. Compete by setting out multiple bags with toys in them. The dog that retrieves an item first, wins!

Create a variation of this game here:

Balls in a Pool
Basic Retrieve

Beginner

Purpose: challenge, retrieval in high distraction

What you will need: baby plastic pool, multi-colored child's plastic fun balls, retrieval items

Instructions:
1. Use positive reinforcement.
2. Start by placing a toy in the pool, near the edge, on the balls, for the dog to retrieve.
3. Graduate to putting the toy in middle of pool then partially bury it, then fully bury it for the dog to retrieve.
4. If the dog starts playing in the balls bring him out, resit him and start over.
5. Compete by having 2 dogs retrieve from the pool at the same time.
6. The first dog that fetches a pool item and brings back to its Player, wins!

Create a variation of this game here:

Balls in a Pool
Item discrimination

Intermediate

Purpose: challenge, retrieval in high distraction

What you will need: baby plastic pool, multi-colored child's plastic fun balls, retrieval items

Instructions:
1. Use positive reinforcement.
2. Start by placing two toys of equal value in the pool, onto the balls.
3. Direct the dog by yes/no (hot/cold) to pick up the toy you want the dog to retrieve.
4. Graduate to putting many items (up to 5) in the pool and direct the dog to get the item you want him to retrieve.
5. Compete by challenging another Player and dog by the speed of their retrieval and/or the number of items retrieved.

Create a variation of this game here:

Benches

Beginner

Purpose: body awareness, challenge, confidence, position exercise

What you will need: bench

Instructions:
1. Use positive reinforcement.
2. Cue or lure the dog to jump onto a bench.
3. Have the dog do different behaviors on the bench such as "Down", "Stand", "Sit", "Move up", "Back", and "Turn around".
4. At a different time, lure the dog "Under" the bench and to a "Down" as you cue "Under". Drop the lure for a clean "Under".
5. Challenge another Player with a dog to see which dog does the behaviors the fastest.

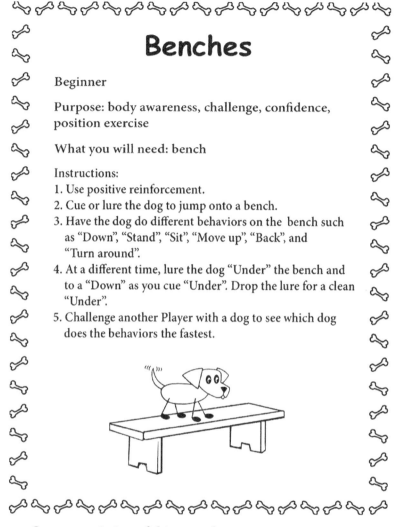

Create a variation of this game here:

Benches
Under

Beginner

Purpose: body awareness, challenge, confidence

What you will need: benches, a row of chairs, or
a row of sawhorses

Instructions:
1. Use positive reinforcement.
2. Line up benches, sawhorses or chairs.
3. Have the dog go "Under" and "Wait".
4. Cue the dog to "Move up", then "Back" by luring.
5. Have the dog retrieve an item while under and
   back out with it.
6. Be creative.
7. Compete against another Player and dog by
   which dog goes "Under" and "Down/Stay" first.

Create a variation of this game here:

Blanket
Bring

Intermediate, Advanced

Purpose: body awareness, challenge, persistence, problem-solving, retrieval

What you will need: blanket or sheet

Instructions:
1. Use positive reinforcement.
2. Dog to have an advanced retrieve.
3. Direct the dog to bring you a sheet or blanket.
4. Let the dog figure out how to get it to you without the dog stepping on it.
5. Compete against another Player and dog.
6. Add difficulty by having the dog pull the item out of a closet or dryer.

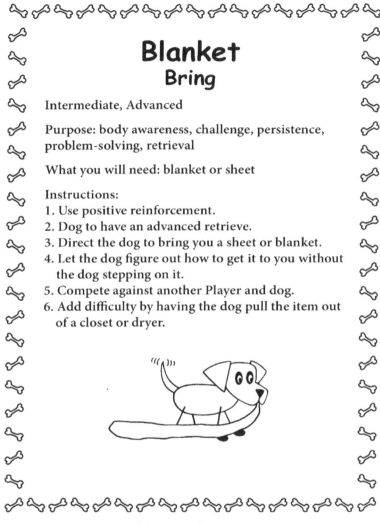

Create a variation of this game here:

Blanket
Hide

Beginner

Purpose: challenge, persistence, problem-solving

What you will need: blanket or sheet

Instructions:
1. Use positive reinforcement.
2. Cover dog completely with a sheet or a blanket.
3. Dog must free itself without encouragement from you.
4. Compete against another Player and dog to see which dog frees itself first.

Create a variation of this game here:

Bow

Intermediate

Purpose: cue exercise, greeting

What you will need: wall

Instructions:
1. Use positive reinforcement.
2. Dog needs a solid "Down" and "Stand".
3. Either stand or sit in a chair.
4. Lure the front end of the dog down while you say, "Bow/Down."
5. Click the bow position, then immediately cue, "Stand" before the dog goes all the way down.
6. Fade the "Down" and "Stand" then just cue, "Bow."
7. If you need more control, teach "Bow" next to a wall to help hold the dog's position.
8. Compete against another Player and dog to see which dog gives the deepest bow.

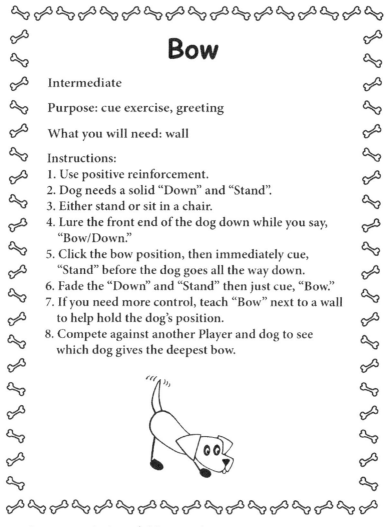

Create a variation of this game here:

Box in Crate

Advanced

Purpose: challenge, persistence, problem-solving, retrieval

What you will need: wire crate, large box

Instructions:
1. Use positive reinforcement.
2. Start with a large box with the flaps open that will fit through the crate door.
3. Dog must retrieve the box out of the crate.
4. Add difficulty by putting more awkward retrieval items in the crate such as a long stick.
5. Compete against another Player and dog to see which dog can pull out the most awkward item.

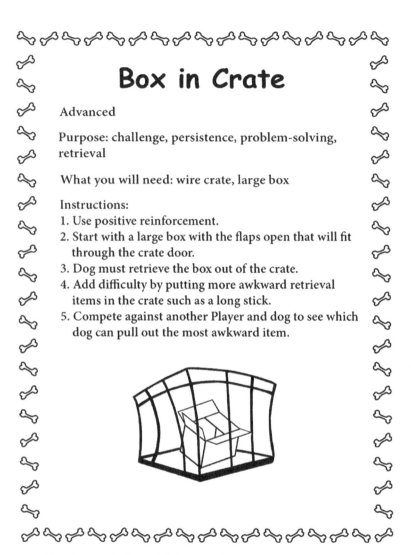

Create a variation of this game here:

Boxes

All levels

Purpose: challenge, persistence, problem-solving, retrieval

What you will need: different sized boxes, retrieval items

Instructions:
1. Use Positive reinforcement.
2. Start with a large box with the flaps open.
3. Dog must retrieve toy out of the box.
4. Graduate to different sized boxes with flaps partially closed.
5. Add more difficult retrieval items.
6. Add difficulty by turning the box on its side or upside down.
7. Challenge the advanced dog by putting one box inside of the other and have the dog separate them to get the retrieval item.
8. Be creative.

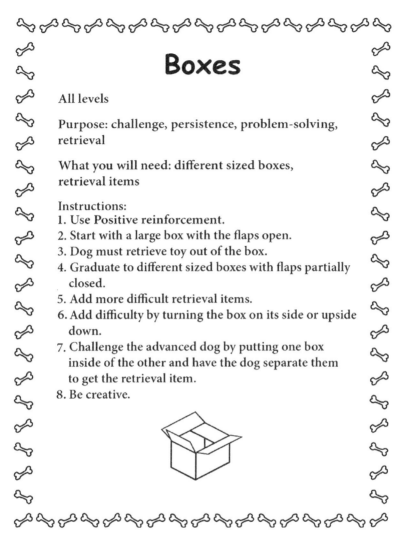

Create a variation of this game here:

Captain, May I?

All levels

Purpose: cue exercise

What you will need: 2 or more players

Instructions:
1. "Captain" turns their back to a line of Players who have dogs.
2. "Captain" calls each Player by name, one at a time, and tells them to take a random number of steps towards him and to have their dogs "Sit" or another position. For example the "Captain" will say "Bobby, take 3 giant steps and have your dog "Sit".
3. Before the Player takes the steps they must ask the "Captain", "Captain, may I?" The "Captain" then answers, "Yes, you may." The Player then takes the steps forward and "Sit" their dog.
4. If the player forgets to ask "Captain, may I?" he must go back to the starting line.
5. The first player to reach the "Captain" gets to be the new "Captain".
6. The number of steps should vary with each Player.

Create a variation of this game here:

Catch
Treat or Toy

Beginner

Purpose: challenge, fun, good way to end a training session, reward, self-control

What you will need: small to medium-sized treats, toy

Instructions:
1. Use positive reinforcement.
2. Have the dog "Sit/Stay".
3. Stand close to the dog.
4. Lure the dog's nose up and drop the treat/toy toward its mouth.
5. Repeat this until the dog catches it.
6. Then take a step back, and gently toss the treat/toy.
7. Do this until the dog reliably catches it and so on.
8. The dog must keep its "Stay". If the dog doesn't catch it, pick it up and try again.
9. Challenge another Player and their dog on how many treats in a row a dog can catch from different distances.

Create a variation of this game here:

Chair Crawl

All levels

Purpose: body awareness, "Under" exercise, self-control

What you will need: 5-6 chairs or more, retrieval items

Instructions:
1. Have the dog "Down/Stay" facing the end of the row of chairs.
2. Lure the dog under the first chair.
3. Drop a treat under each chair.
4. As the dog crawls forward say, "Crawl," then click or mark when the dog snags the treat.
5. Have the dog wait at the end of the chairs before cuing the dog out.
6. Add difficulty by having the dog crawl backwards through the row of chairs and exit at the starting point.
7. Add difficulty by having a retrieval item at the end of the crawl for the dog to retrieve and bring out from under the chairs.
8. Compete with another Player by setting up another row of chairs.

Create a variation of this game here:

Chicken Walk

Beginner

Purpose: challenge, recall, self-control

What you will need: 10 small pieces of chicken wrapped in 10 paper towels

Instructions:
1. Use positive reinforcement.
2. Scatter the food balls around the floor or parking lot.
3. Dogs are on leash, walking around and near the balls.
4. When dog shows interest in the food ball, cue dog to a "Here".
5. When dog looks at you and leaves the food ball alone, reward.
6. When a dog goes for a food ball they are out of the game.

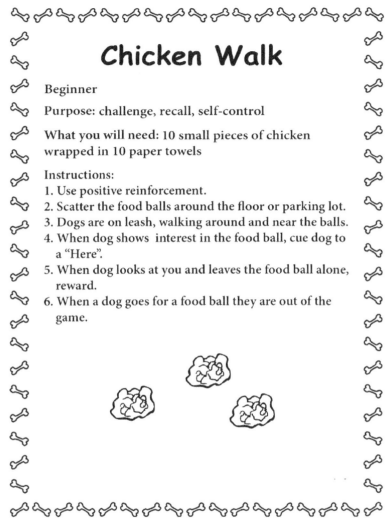

Create a variation of this game here:

Clean Your Room

Advanced

Purpose: teaching "Put". Used for putting toys in a box, trash in a trash can, cans in a recycle bin and so on.

What you will need: low box, dog toys, clicker and treats

Instructions:
1. Use positive reinforcement.
2. Dog needs a solid retrieve and "Drop".
3. Place a few toys next to a box on the floor.
4. Have the dog retrieve a toy.
5. Cue "Put/Drop" as you lift the box under the dog's mouth.
6. Reward when the toy drops into the box.
7. Repeat. Extinguish "Drop".
8. Graduate to leaving the box on the floor close to the dog.
9. Graduate to adding distance between the dog and the box.
10. Compete by timing how fast each dog puts the toys away!

Create a variation of this game here:

Coat Tree

Intermediate to Advanced

Purpose: challenge, persistence, retrieval

What you will need: treats, coat tree, retrieval items to hang on the tree, kitchen step-ladder

Instructions:
1. Use positive reinforcement.
2. Dog must have an advanced retrieve.
3. Teach the dog to step on the ladder separately first. (Page 46)
4. Hang something on the coat tree you know the dog will retrieve, then have the dog go up the step-ladder to retrieve the item.
5. Challenge each dog to retrieve more and more difficult items off the tree.

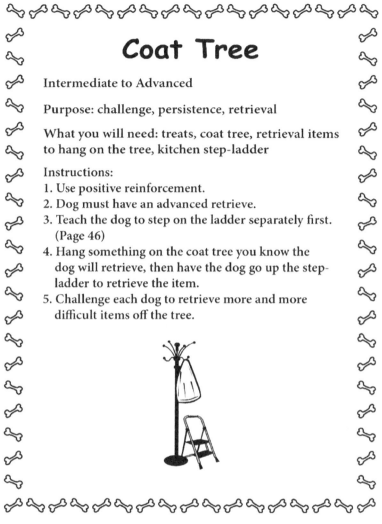

Create a variation of this game here:

Cones
Scent

Beginner

Purpose: challenge, persistence, scent discrimination

What you will need: high-value food, high-value toy, plastic cones

Instructions:
1. Line up 6 or more cones.
2. Hide a piece of food under one of them.
3. Direct your dog to "Search".
4. Let your dog use his nose to find the goodie.
5. Dog to move the cone to get the goodie.
   Repeat by using a favorite toy.
6. Let the dog sniff the toy, then hide the toy under a cone.
7. Dog to find and retrieve it.
8. Each Player to challenge another Player's dog to find something the first Player hid under a cone.

Create a variation of this game here:

Cue Train

Intermediate, Advanced

Purpose: cue exercise

What you will need: 2 or more players

Instructions:
1. Use positive reinforcement.
2. Player #1 gives their dog a cue to perform.
3. Player #2 repeats Player #1's cue then adds one more.
4. Player #3 repeats Player #1 and #2's cues in same the order, then adds one more.
5. The goal is to remember the string of cues in the original order.
6. When a Player misses a cue or changes the order of the cues that player is out.

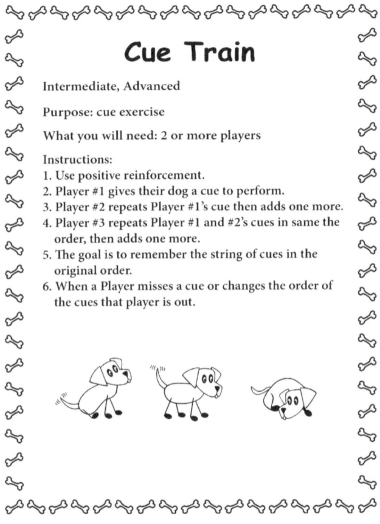

Create a variation of this game here:

Cupboard Fun

Beginner

Purpose: challenge, confidence in small dark places, retrieval

What you will need: cupboard loaded with plastic containers or pans, desired toy

Instructions:
1. Use positive reinforcement.
2. Show the dog a toy and toss it deep into the cupboard.
3. Cue the dog to "Get it" and "Bring" it to you.
4. Graduate to other retrieval items.

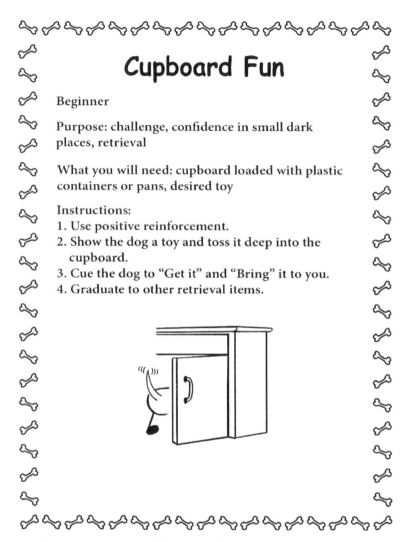

Create a variation of this game here:

Cups with Water

Beginner

Purpose: exercise to train dog to walk on a loose leash, self-control

What you will need: small cup filled almost to the top with water

Instructions:
1. Players hold a cup of water in the opposite hand of the hand holding the leash.
2. Walk the dogs in a low distraction area.
3. Players to keep the dog's attention by changing directions, etc.
4. Increase distractions as the Players successfully walk with a loose leash with no spilling of water.
5. Add difficulty by repeating 1-4 but hold the cup of water with the same hand that is holding the leash.
6. Players that spill water are out of the game.
7. Add fun by making this game a relay race.

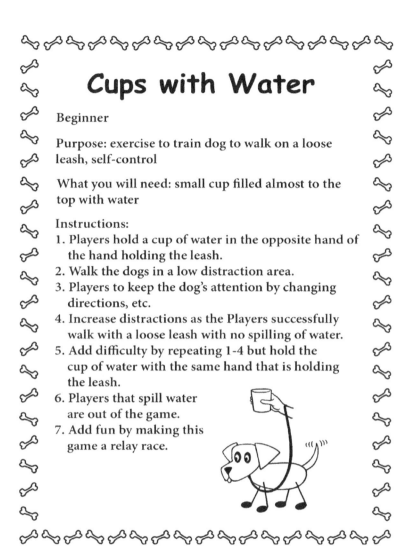

Create a variation of this game here:

Distance Here

Beginner

Purpose: recall exercise

What you will need: treats

Instructions:
1. Start with the dog a few feet away.
2. Hold a treat in your fist. (Hand signal, Page 34)
3. Show the dog your fist with a treat in it and cue, "Here" (Come).
4. Slowly drop your fist to your thigh as the dog runs to you.
5. When the dog gets to you, give the "Sit" hand signal and give the dog the treat.
6. Graduate to further distances from the dog with variable treating.
7. The farther away the dog, the higher you raise your fist.
8. When proficient, extinguish the treat.
9. Challenge other Players on the speed of their dogs at different distances.

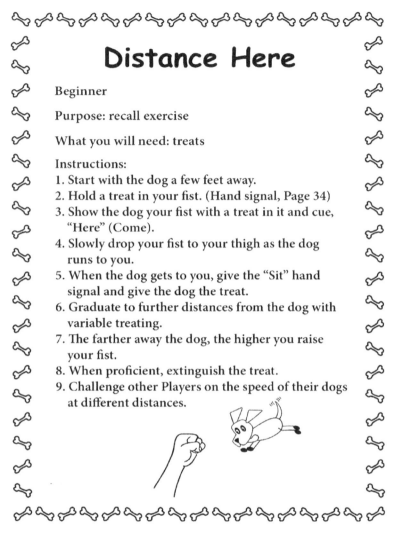

Create a variation of this game here:

Dogs in the Middle

All levels

Purpose: cue exercise, self-control

What you will need: group of dogs

Instructions:
1. Have a group of dogs lay close to each other in a "Down/Stay".
2. The dogs must ignore each other.
3. The Players circle the group of dogs.
4. Two of the Players cue their dog to "Sit/Stay". while the other dogs keep their "Down/Stay".
5. After 30-60 seconds cue the sitting dogs to "Down/Stay", then cue two of the "Down/Stay" dogs to "Sit/Stay" and so on.
6. Add difficulty by folding in "Stand/Stay".
7. When a Player's dog breaks a "Stay" that dog is out of the game.

Create a variation of this game here:

Down on the Spot

All levels

Purpose: teaching the dog to go down on a specific spot

What you will need: treats, 5 small mats or bathroom rugs, 3 players

Instructions:
1. Use positive reinforcement.
2. Spread 5 mats around the room.
3. Each Player points to a mat and says their dog's name, then "Down/Stay".
4. Have the dog "Stay" for 30 seconds or more.
5. Each Player then points to an empty mat and repeats. Do this 5 times.
6. Extinguish the "Down/Stay" and just point at an empty mat when saying the dog's name to have the dog move to a new mat.
7. When a dog breaks the "Down/Stay' then that Player is out of the game.

Create a variation of this game here:

Dunkin' for Treats

Beginner

Purpose: challenge, persistence, retrieval

What you will need: treats that float and don't float (first use a high-value treat like hot dogs), large bucket or plastic pool

Instructions:
1. Fill a container with water.
2. Drop treats into the container. Let the dog have at it!

Create a variation of this game here:

Easy Button

Intermediate

Purpose: cue exercise, teaching "Paw" or "Touch" (nose)

What you will need: treats, 3 Easy Buttons from Staples

Instructions:
1. Use positive reinforcement.
2. Decide whether you want the dog to trigger the button with a paw ("Paw") or a nose ("Touch"). (Page 62)
3. Shape this behavior, then add the cue "Paw" or "Touch" cue.
4. Set 3 Easy Buttons on the floor. Time how long it takes for each dog to trigger all 3. The best time wins!

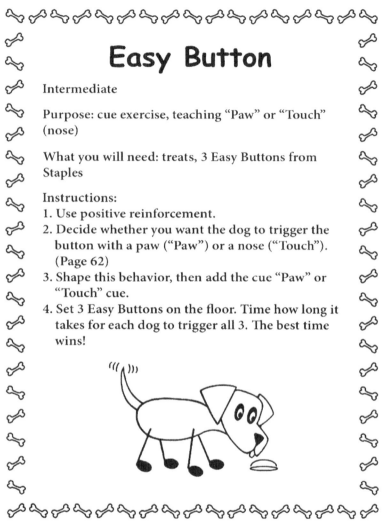

Create a variation of this game here:

Easy Button
as a Reward

Intermediate

Purpose: cue exercise, teaching the dog to combine
behaviors (chain)

What you will need: Easy Button from Staples

Instructions:
1. Teach the Easy button separately. (Page 25)
2. After the dog successfully completes a behavior,
   instruct him to trigger the Easy button. Reward.
3. Extinguish the reward.
4. Use the Easy button as the reward.

Bow   Reward

Create a variation of this game here:

Egg

Intermediate, Advanced

Purpose: challenge, retrieval, self-control

What you will need: one hard boiled egg, one raw egg, dozen eggs in a carton

Instructions:
1. Use positive reinforcement.
2. Have the dog "Sit/Stay".
3. Have the dog take a hard boiled egg from your hand and hold briefly.
4. Have the dog put the egg back into your hand.
5. Put the hard boiled egg on the floor.
6. Have the dog pick up the egg and put it in your hand.
7. Once proficient, where the dog does not crack the egg shell and gives it back to your hand whole, repeat with a raw egg.
8. Put an egg carton on the floor filled with 12 raw eggs. (You can use blown eggs too.)
9. The Player's dog that picks the most eggs out of the carton, non-cracked, and puts in your hand wins!

Create a variation of this game here:

27

Eye Contact

Beginner

Purpose: eye contact exercise between person and dog

What you will need: treats

Instructions:
1. Use positive reinforcement.
2. Sit the dog in front of you, facing you.
3. Have a treat in each hand.
4. When the dog looks you in the eye instead of at a hand with the treat, reward.
5. Slowly increase the time the dog spends looking at your eyes before treating.

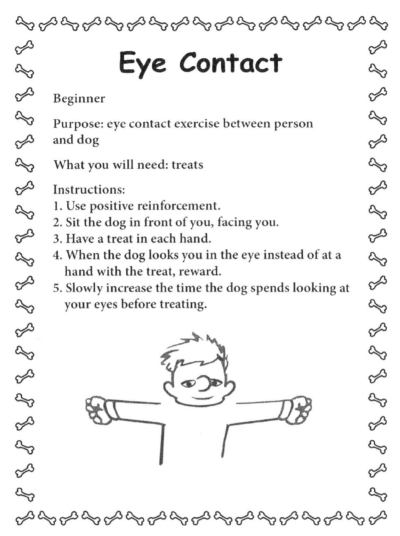

Create a variation of this game here:

Finders Keepers

All levels

Purpose: challenge, retrieval, scent discrimination

What you will need: small plastic containers, treats

Instructions:
1. Use positive reinforcement.
2. Put a treat in each container.
3. Hide the containers around an area or room.
4. Cue the dog to "Search".
5. When the dog finds a container cue, "Bring".
6. When the dog brings it to you dramatically open the container and give the dog the treat.
7. Send the dog out to search for another container.

Create a variation of this game here:

Flip a Coin

All levels

Purpose: exercise in behaviors

What you will need: coin(s)

Instructions:
1. One Player filps a coin and another Player calls heads or tails.
2. The Player that wins the toss tells the losing Player what behavior their dog must demonstrate.

Create a variation of this game here:

Follow the Leader

All levels

Purpose: cue exercise

What you will need: treats

Instructions:
1. Use positive reinforcement.
2. Two or more Players.
3. Players make a line, front to back, with their dogs.
4. The Player first in line, Leader, has their dog do a behavior.
5. Like falling dominoes, the next player does the same behavior, then the next, then the next and so on.
6. After the last Player's dog does the Leader's behavior, the Leader falls back to the end of the line and second in line is now the Leader.
7. Follow the leader again having the dogs do a new behavior and so on.
8. Repeat until all Players have a chance to be a Leader.

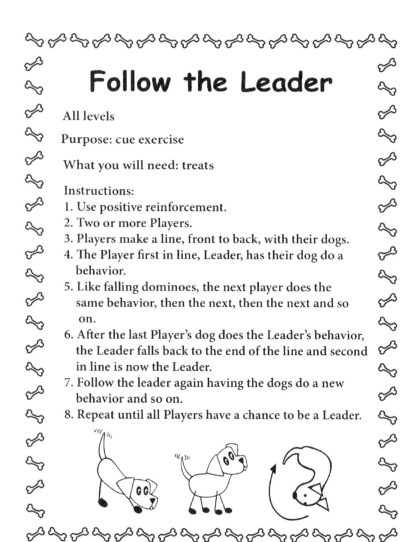

Create a variation of this game here:

Food Court

All levels

Purpose: challenge, recall, self-control

What you will need: treats, different bits of food, 2 or more Players

Instructions:

1. Use positive reinforcement.
2. In a large area place different bits of food on things, under things, and out in the open. Find some food wrappers out of the trash. The gooier the better.
3. Each Player walks around the area with their dog on a loose leash.
4. The Players randomly have their dogs "Sit" and "Down".
5. If the dog looks at the food call the dog to a "Here" to get its eyes back on you.
6. If a dog snags a bit of food that team is out of the game.
7. Next, line up the dogs on one side of the area in a "Sit/Stay".
8. Players line up at the opposite side of the area.
9. Each Player recalls their dog to a "Here" (come).
10. The dog that stops to snack is out of the game.
11. Repeat.

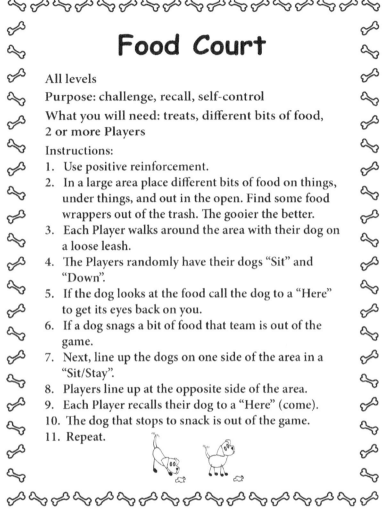

Create a variation of this game here:

Hand Signal Challenge

All levels

Purpose: cue exercise, teaching the dog to watch you by using hand signals

What you will need: treats, 2 or more players

Instructions:
1. Use positive reinforcement.
2. Teach a hand signal by pairing it with the word cue. Extinguish the word cue.
3. Challenge another Player to direct their dog with 3 or more hand signals. (Pages 34-38) (Use your own hand signals if you have some.)
4. Use the dog's name to get its attention first before cuing with the hand signal.
5. The Player that directs their dog with the most hand signals wins!

Create a variation of this game here:

Hand Signals

Back: Flick your fingers away from your body.

Distance here: Hold fist up then slowly bring to your side as dog gets closer.

Down/Chill: Point where you want the dog to down.

Follow: Point behind you.

Create a variation of this game here:

Hand Signals

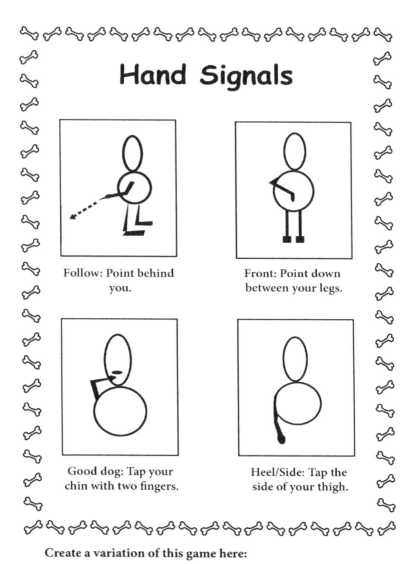

Follow: Point behind you.

Front: Point down between your legs.

Good dog: Tap your chin with two fingers.

Heel/Side: Tap the side of your thigh.

Create a variation of this game here:

Hand Signals

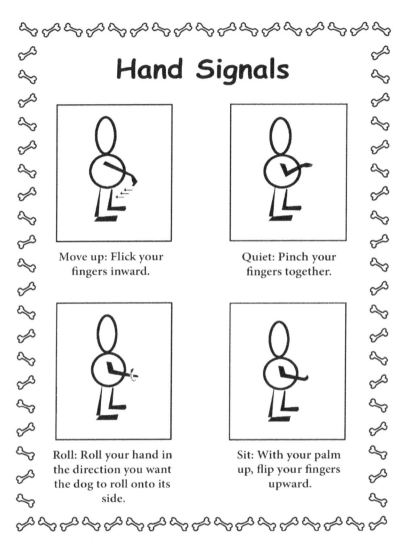

Move up: Flick your fingers inward.

Quiet: Pinch your fingers together.

Roll: Roll your hand in the direction you want the dog to roll onto its side.

Sit: With your palm up, flip your fingers upward.

Create a variation of this game here:

Hand Signals

Speak: With your palm out, flare your fingers.

Stand: With your palm inward, move your forearm and hand straight up.

Stay: Stop sign at the wrist.

Spin: Point your finger down and twirl it.

Create a variation of this game here:

Hand Signals

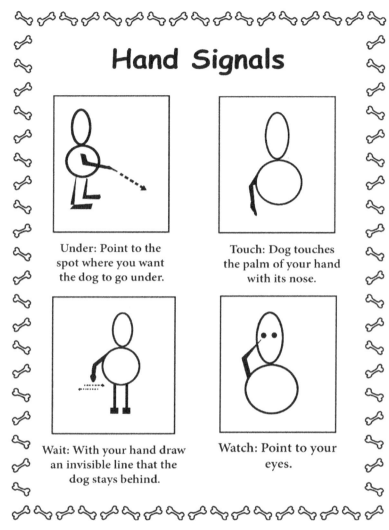

Under: Point to the spot where you want the dog to go under.

Touch: Dog touches the palm of your hand with its nose.

Wait: With your hand draw an invisible line that the dog stays behind.

Watch: Point to your eyes.

Create a variation of this game here:

Hide 'n Seek
Bush or House

Beginner

Purpose: challenge, persistence, problem-solving, retrieval

What you will need: dog toy, 3 or more dogs

Instructions:
1. Hide dog toys in bushes and trees.
2. Off leash, let the dogs find and retrieve the toys.
3. The dog that fetches the most toys wins!

Create a variation of this game here:

Hide 'n Seek
Person

Intermediate

Purpose: challenge, persistence, problem-solving, recall, retrieval

What you will need: hiding place

Instructions:
1. Put the dog in a "Down/Stay".
2. The person hides.
3. The hiding person calls the dog.
4. When the dog finds the person give a reward.

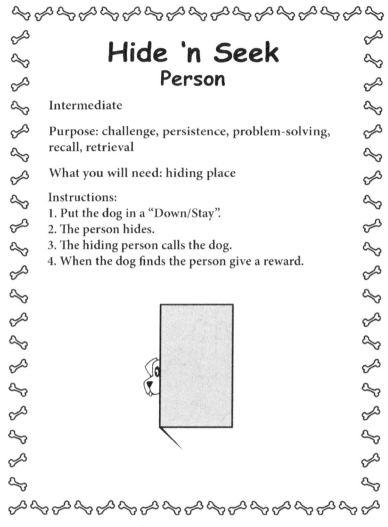

Create a variation of this game here:

High Five

Beginner

Purpose: greeting exercise

What you will need: treats

Instructions:
1. Use positive reinforcement.
2. Dog needs a solid "Shake".
3. Cue, "High five/Shake."
4. When the dog lifts its paw turn your hand to a high five position.
5. Reward when the paw hits the high five position.
6. Extinguish "Shake".
7. Use only "High-five".

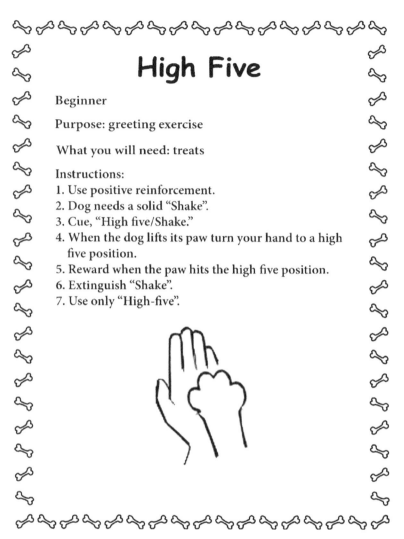

Create a variation of this game here:

Hot/Cold

All levels

Purpose: retrieval exercise, self-control

What you will need: treats, retrieval items

Instructions:
1. Use positive reinforcement.
2. Dog needs to know how to retrieve and "Look" for an item. (Page 52)
3. Start with 2 equally valuable items on the floor, about 1' apart.
4. Predetermine in your mind which item you want the dog to retrieve.
5. Cue the dog to "Look".
6. As the dog approaches the items, cue the dog "Yes" or "No" to direct the dog to the item you want him to retrieve.
7. Cue the dog to "Get it" when his nose strikes the right object.
8. Have the dog bring you the item and drop it on the floor or put it in your hand.
9. If the dog brings you the wrong item, thank him and send him out again to get the correct item.
10. Once proficient with 2 items add more items and items of different values.

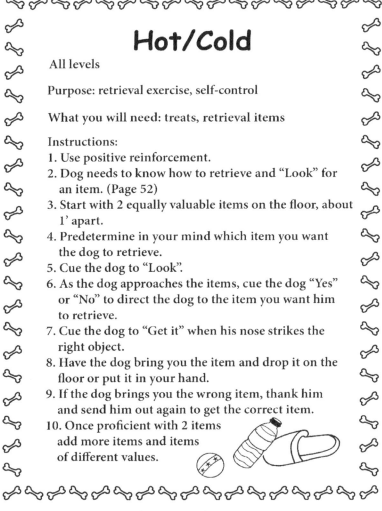

Create a variation of this game here:

Hot Potato

All levels

Purpose: challenge, cue exercise, self-control

What you will need: potatoes or tennis balls, 2 or more Players

Instructions:
1. All Players are standing in a circle.
2. The dogs are in a "Down/Stay".
3. One Player has a potato and tosses it to another Player and so on.
4. If a dog breaks its "Stay" then they are out of the game.
5. Also, try this game where all the Players sitting in chairs with their dogs in a "Sit/Stay" next to them.
6. For difficulty, add a second potato so 2 are in the air.

Create a variation of this game here:

Hot Potato
Loose Leash

All levels

Purpose: exercise for loose leash walking, self-control

What you will need: potatoes, 2 or more Players

Instructions:
1. One person has the potato.
2. All Players go for a walk with their dogs, close enough to each other so that a potato can be tossed and caught by another Player.
3. Dog that tries to get the potato while in the air is out of the game.

Create a variation of this game here:

Jinx

Beginner

Purpose: cue exercise

What you will need: treats, stack of cards with different cues written on them

Instructions:
1. Use positive reinforcement.
2. A Player in the group picks a card out of the stack and shows it to the rest of the Players.
3. All Players cue their dogs on what was written on the card.
4. If a Player does not use the dog's name before giving the cue then they are *jinxed* and out of the game.

Create a variation of this game here:

Ladder

Intermediate to Advanced

Purpose: body awareness, challenge, retrieval

What you will need: kitchen step-ladder, something on a shelf or box

Instructions:
1. Use positive reinforcement.
2. Dog to have retrieval skills.
3. Teach the dog to go up onto the ladder separately.
4. Place the dog's favorite item on a shelf above the ladder.
5. Encourage the dog to retrieve it.
6. Compete with other Players and their dogs on which dog retrieves the most difficult item.

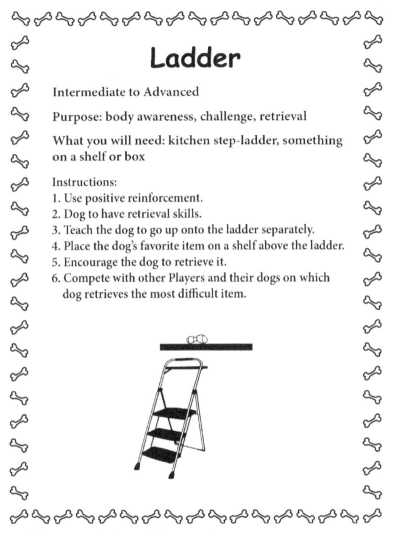

Create a variation of this game here:

Ladder
Flat

Beginner

Purpose: body awareness, challenge

What you will need: 8' to 10' ladder

Instructions:
1. Lay the ladder flat on the ground, against a wall.
2. On leash have the dog walk slowly between the rungs.
3. When the dog has confidence going forward, have the dog walk slowly backwards over the rungs.
4. For more difficulty, at the same time have one dog walking forward as a second dog walks backwards over the rungs.

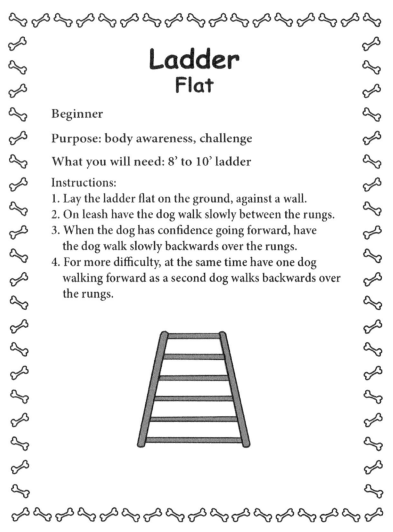

Create a variation of this game here:

Laundry

Advanced

Purpose: challenge, persistence, retrieval

What you will need: laundry basket, clothes dryer, clothes

Instructions:
1. Use positive reinforcement.
2. Dog needs to know "Get it" and "Put" (Drop). (Page 74)
3. Place the laundry basket next to the dryer.
4. Cue the dog to "Get it", an item out of the dryer, and "Put" into the basket.

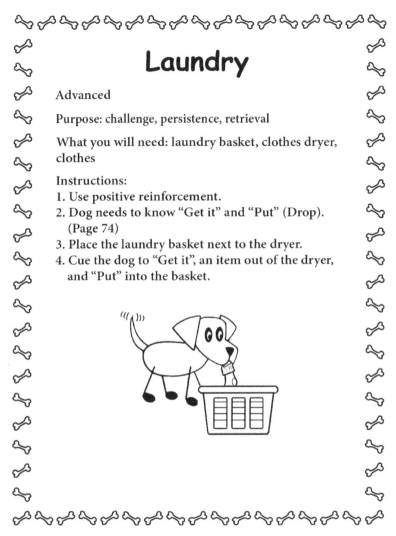

Create a variation of this game here:

Laundry Basket
Train

All levels

Purpose: body awareness, challenge, confidence, retrieval, self-control

What you will need: 5 laundry baskets, bungee cords to link them together, odds and ends to put into each basket, 2 boundaries to keep the dog moving along the train such as an x-pen and a wall

Instructions:
1. Link the baskets together with the bungee cords.
2. Put baskets on the floor against a wall with an opened x-pen along the other side.
3. Put different things in the bottom of the baskets such as empty cans, bubble wrap, crinkled paper, etc.
4. On leash, encourage the dog to walk through the baskets.
5. Once comfortable, do off leash. Put a toy at the end of the train for the dog to retrieve and bring back to you.

Create a variation of this game here:

Laundry Basket
& Ball

Beginner

Purpose: challenge, persistence, problem-solving, retrieval

What you will need: laundry basket, ball or dog toy

Instructions:
1. Use positive reinforcement.
2. Turn laundry basket upside down.
3. Put a ball or dog toy under the basket.
4. Let the dog figure out how to get the item from under the basket.
5. The Player's dog that retrieves the item the fastest wins.

Create a variation of this game here:

Leap Frog

All levels

Purpose: cue exercise, self-control

What you will need: Players with dogs

Instructions:
1. Have 3 or more dogs lay in a row about 5' apart.
2. The last dog in the row dog steps or jumps over all the dogs in the row then lays down.
3. The next dog in the row repeats and so on.
4. Add challenge by doing different positions.
5. If the dogs can't jump over another dog they can go around.
6. Add target mats if you need them.

Create a variation of this game here:

Look

All levels

Purpose: challenge, teaches the dog to look on the floor for an item (dog will already have retrieval skills)

What you will need: treats, retrieval items

Instructions:
1. Use positive reinforcement.
2. Have the dog "Sit/Stay".
3. Show the dog a toy then put the toy on the floor.
4. Cue the dog to "Look".
5. When the dog touches the toy have the dog fetch it and put it in your hand.
6. Now put 2 toys on the floor. Decide in advance which toy you want the dog to retrieve.
7. Cue the dog to "Look". Use the yes/no (hot/cold) game to direct the dog to the right item to retrieve. (Page 42)
8. If the dog retrieves the wrong item "Thank" him for the item then send him back out to retrieve the item you want.
9. Increase the challenge by adding more toys or household items for the dog to "Look" for.
10. Scatter many retrieval items around the room. Invite other Players with dogs to "Look" for the same predetermined item.
11. The dog that finds that particular item wins.

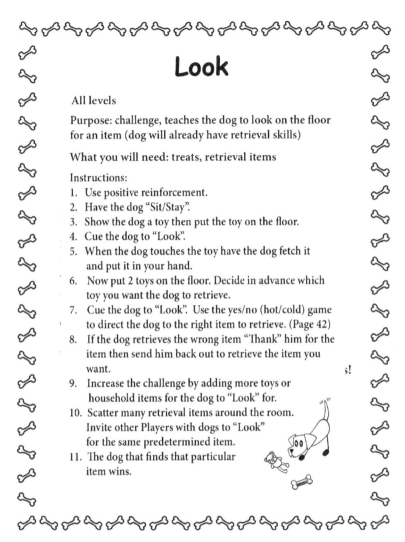

Create a variation of this game here:

Look Up

Intermediate, Advanced

Purpose: retrieval exercise, teaches the dog to look up onto a counter or table for an item to retrieve (dog will already have retrieval skills)

What you will need: treats, retrieval items

Instructions:
1. Use positive reinforcement.
2. Put a favorite toy on a table near the edge where the dog can see it.
3. Have the dog sit in front of the table.
4. Cue "Look up" as you point to the toy.
5. When the dog looks up at the toy, reward.
6. Cue the dog to get it and put it in your hand.
7. Put the toy in different up places and repeat.
8. Add more interesting items.
9. Compete with other Players by scattering different items around the room, up on tables, chairs, etc.
10. The dog that retrieves the most wins!
11. Now yo-yo the dog between "Look" and "Look up" by putting objects around the room, some up, some on the floor.

Create a variation of this game here:

Maze 1

All levels

Purpose: challenge, confidence, problem-solving, recall

What you will need: a number of X-pens, bungee cords

Instructions:
1. Configure the x-pens into a maze.
2. Have an opening in 2 places.
3. Player 1 will place Player 2's dog in a "Sit/Stay" at one opening.
4. Player 2 will stand next to the second opening and call their dog.
5. If the dog can't figure out how to get to their person, then simplify the maze.

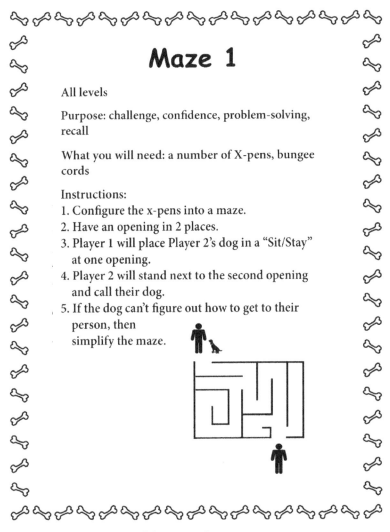

Create a variation of this game here:

Maze 2

Intermediate

Purpose: challenge, confidence, problem-solving, recall

What you will need: a number of X-pens, chair, small table

Instructions:
1. Build a maze.
2. In one part of the maze put a chair where the dog has to figure out how to get past it to get to you.
3. Put a small table and chair in the maze where the dog has to go under or over it to get to you.

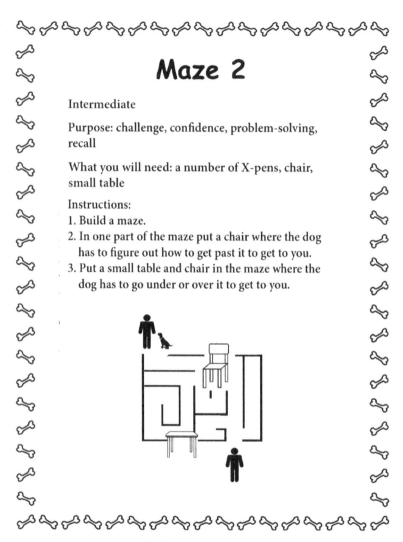

Create a variation of this game here:

Maze 3

Intermediate, Advanced

Purpose: challenge, confidence, problem-solving, recall, retrieval

What you will need: a number of X-pens, retrieval item

Instructions:
1. Build a maze.
2. Near the exit of the maze put a retrieval item.
3. Before the dog exits have the dog pick up the item and bring it to you after the dog exits.
4. Add a challenge by putting a container just outside the exit and have the dog "Put" (drop) the item into the container. (Page 74)

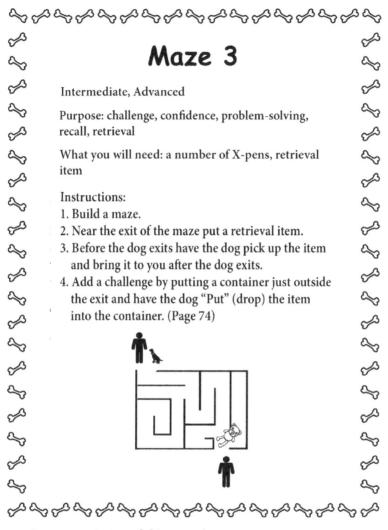

Create a variation of this game here:

Maze 4

Advanced

Purpose: challenge, confidence, problem-solving, retrieval

What you will need: a number of X-pens, chair, small table, retrieval item

Instructions:
1. Build a maze.
2. In one part of the maze put a chair where the dog has to figure out how to get past it to get to you.
3. Put a small table in the maze where the dog has to go under or over it to get to you.
4. Add a retrieval item. Have the dog pick it up and bring to you.
5. Be creative.

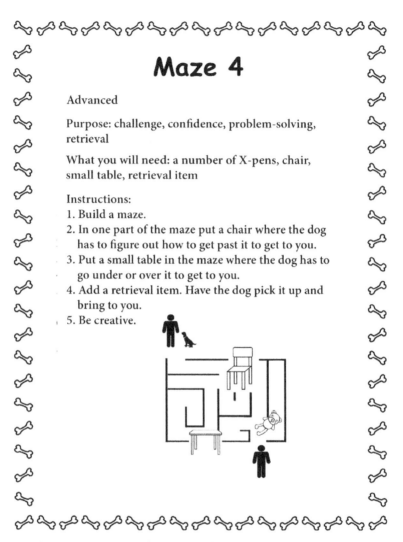

Create a variation of this game here:

Musical Chairs

All levels

Purpose: cue exercise, immediate response
to cues

What you will need: 6 chairs, 7 players, music and
dogs with a solid "Heel", "Side", "Down", "Sit" ,"Stand"
and "Stay"

Instructions:
1. Put the chairs in a circle with the seats facing out.
2. Players are told before the music starts if the dog is to
   be in a heel or side (opposite of heel) while circling
   the chairs, and if the dogs are to "Sit", "Down" or
   "Stand" when the music stops.
3. When the music stops the Player sits in the nearest
   chair then cues the dog to the predetermined position.
4. Team that doesn't capture a chair is out.
5. If a Player captures a chair but the dog doesn't hold
   the designated position until the music starts again,
   the team is out.

Create a variation of this game here:

Musical Hula Hoops

All levels

Purpose: cue exercise, immediate response to cues

What you will need: treats and clicker, 6 hula hoops, 5 to 7 players, music

Instructions:
1. It is a doggie cake walk.
2. There are more Players than hoops.
3. Dogs need a solid "Heel", "Side", "Down", "Sit" and "Stand".
4. Players are instructed to circle the group of hoops with their dogs in a "Heel".
5. Play music while they are circling.
6. Tell all that when the music stops that each dog has to immediately go into a hoop and "Sit/Stay". (Change to other positions to keep the game interesting.)
7. Team that doesn't capture a hoop and/or hold the pre-announced position in the hoop, is out of the game.

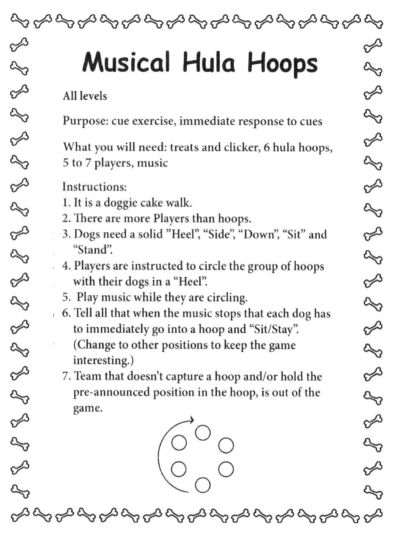

Create a variation of this game here:

Parkour
Indoor

All levels

Purpose: body awareness, challenge, confidence

What you will need: large indoor area with items
that the dog can go on, around, under or through

Instructions:
1. On leash (off leash if safe).
2. Encourage the dog to take full advantage of the
   indoor obstacles such as items for the dog to go
   around, under, in and on.

Create a variation of this game here:

Parkour
Outdoor

All levels

Purpose: body awareness, challenge, confidence

What you will need: open area where dog can go on, around, under or through something

Instructions:
1. On leash (off leash if safe) encourage the dog to take full advantage of an environment.
2. Find objects or places where the dog can go around, under, through and on.

Create a variation of this game here:

Paw or Touch

All levels

Purpose: challenge, cue discrimination, problem-solving

What you will need: treats, touch stick, Frisbee

Instructions:
1. Use positive reinforcement.
2. Teach "Touch" and "Paw" separately using the target stick for "Touch" and the Frisbee for "Paw".
3. When proficient put the touch stick and the Frisbee behind your back.
4. Show the dog one at a time and give the appropriate cue.
5. For the advanced dog put away the touch stick and just use the Frisbee. The dog will be cued to "Touch" or "Paw" the Frisbee only.
6. Compete against other Players and dogs by putting 6 items on the floor. Each Player cues the their dog to "Touch" or "Paw" each item. The dog that gets the most right wins!

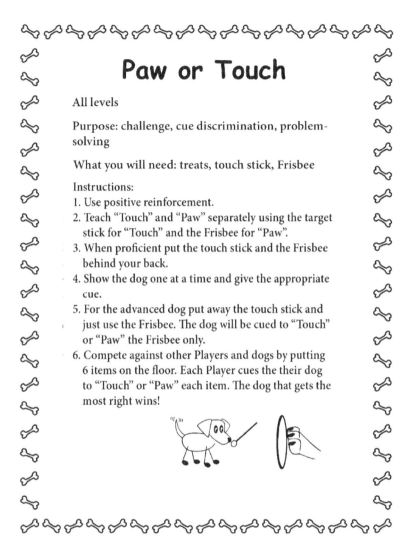

Create a variation of this game here:

Ping-pong Balls and Spoons

Beginner

Purpose: exercise for loose leash walking, self-control

What you will need: spoons, ping-pong balls

Instructions:
1. Make a start and finish line.
2. Dogs are on leash.
3. Players hold a spoon that is balancing a ping-pong ball with the non-leash hand.
4. Goal is to walk the dog without the ping-pong ball falling off the spoon.
5. First Player across the finish line wins.
6. Repeat but put the spoon and ping-pong ball in the hand holding the leash.

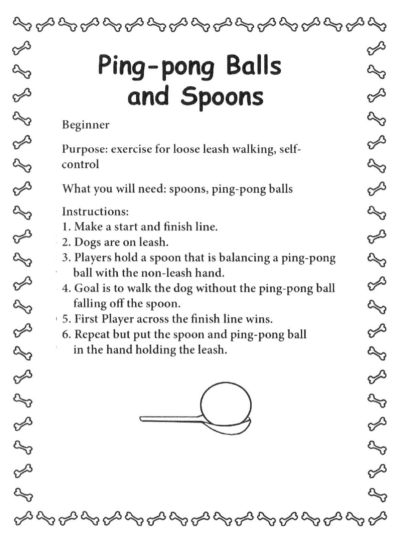

Create a variation of this game here:

Ping-Pong
Deliver

Advanced

Purpose: cue exercise, delivering an item to another person (dog needs retrieval skills)

What you will need: treats, 2 or more Players, retrieval items

Instructions:
1. Use positive reinforcement.
2. Start with a small circle of Players (or just 2).
3. Players stand a few feet apart from each other. Add distance as the dog gets better at the game.
4. One Player gives their dog an item then points to another Player and cues the dog to "Deliver".
5. Within a second of the cue "Deliver" the other Player cues, "Here" (come).
6. When the dog delivers the item, the Player receiving the item, rewards.

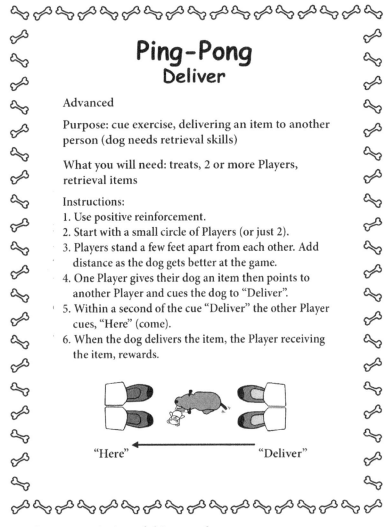

"Here" ⟵———————————— "Deliver"

Create a variation of this game here:

Ping-Pong
Positions

All levels

Purpose: cue and recall exercise

What you will need: treats, 2 or more Players

Instructions:
1. Use positive reinforcement.
2. Start with a small circle of Players (or just 2).
3. One Player does not have a dog.
4. All other Players have their dog in a "Heel/Sit/Stay".
5. Player without a dog calls another Player's dog by name then "Here" (come).
6. When the dog comes to the caller, the caller cues the dog to a "Heel".
7. The Player without a dog calls another Player's dog as in 3 & 4.
8. As the dogs get more reliable increase the distance between people and add more positions.

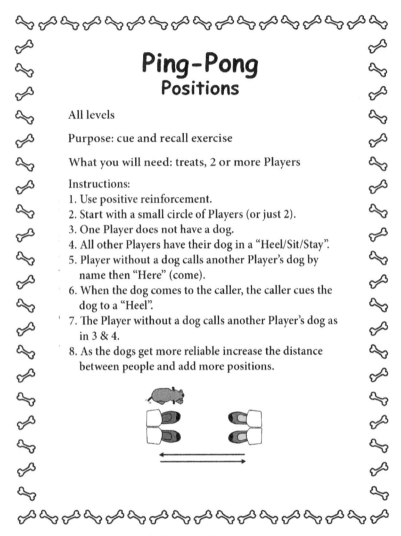

Create a variation of this game here:

Ping-Pong
Race

All levels

Purpose: cue exercise, game, recall

What you will need: treats and clicker, 2 or more Players

Instructions:
1. Start with a small circle of Players (or just 2).
2. Players exchange dogs.
3. Have the dogs "Sit/Stay" in a "Heel" or "Side".
4. At the same time all Players call their dog.
5. When the dog comes to the caller, have the dog "Sit", click-treat.
6. As the dog gets more reliable increase the distance between Players.
7. Add difficulty by having the dog finish in a "Side", "Heel", "Front" or "Follow".

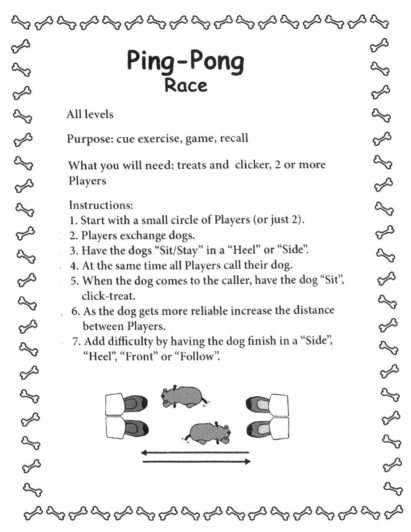

Create a variation of this game here:

Ping Pong
Recall

All levels

Purpose: cue exercise, foundation for "Deliver" and "Get help", recall

What you will need: treats, 2 or more Players

Instructions:
1. Use positive reinforcement.
2. Start with a small circle of Players (or just 2).
3. One at a time each person calls another Player's dog to "Here" (come).
4. When the dog comes to the caller, have the dog sit, click-treat.
5. As the dog gets more reliable increase the distance between people.
6. Increase the speed of the recall with high value treats and a party voice.

Create a variation of this game here:

Player Challenge

All levels

Purpose: challenge, fun, game, player innovation

What you will need: anything you can find in your environment

Instructions:
1. One Player challenges another Player to try something new with their dog, such as retrieve an unusual item or demonstrate unusual combinations of dog positions or both. Be creative.
2. Each Player gets to challenge another.

Create a variation of this game here:

Playing Cards

All levels

Purpose: cue exercise

What you will need: treats and clicker, playing cards

Instructions:
1. Have each Player pull a card out of the deck.
2. Face cards and Jokers are free cards. The Player holding one of these cards tells another Player what cues they have to demonstrate with their dog.
3. Players with numbered cards have to demonstrate as many cues as the numbers on the card.

Create a variation of this game here:

Poling

Beginner

Purpose: challenge, awareness of Player, problem-solving

What you will need: poles that you find in the environment or man made poles on a stand

Instructions:
1. Use positive reinforcement.
2. On leash walk the dog up to an anchored pole and suddenly step around it.
3. The dog should follow you.
4. If the dog doesn't follow you, it will get the leash hung up on the pole.
5. If the leash is hung up on the pole, stand still until the dog backs up and goes the direction you are going.
6. Line up 6 or more poles and challenge other Players and their dogs to weave through them.
7. The first Player that weaves around the poles without getting the leash caught wins.

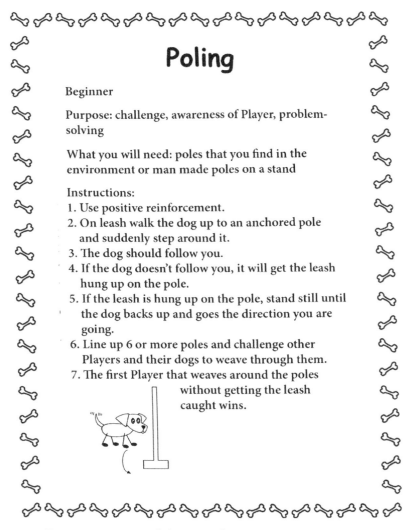

Create a variation of this game here:

Pots

Intermediate, Advanced

Purpose: challenge, metal retrieval, persistence, problem-solving

What you will need: pots of different sizes with lids, treats and/or toys

Instructions:
1. Use positive reinforcement.
2. Put treat or toy in a pot with the lid on.
3. Encourage the dog to lift the lid by the knob to get the treat/toy.
4. Then have the dog bring you the lid and the pot.
5. Challenge other Players and their dogs by putting 5 pots with lids on the floor.
6. Put a treat or toy in one of the pots.
7. The dog that finds the toy or treat on the first try and takes the lid off the pot wins!

Create a variation of this game here:

Puppy Push-ups

All levels

Purpose: cue exercise

What you will need: dog

Instructions:
1. Players cue their dog 3 behaviors such as "Sit", "Stand", "Down" in the first round.
2. In the second round Players repeat their first string of cues and add one more cue, now 4.
3. In the third round Players even add one more cue, now 5. And so on.
4. When a Player's dog doesn't do the cue asked that team is out.
5. Last team standing, wins!

Create a variation of this game here:

Push

Beginner

Purpose: challenge, to move a large object or push a door open

What you will need: empty 5 gallon water bottle, medium-sized box with something heavy in it, door

Instructions:
1. Use positive reinforcement.
2. Teach the dog to push at the bottom of an object for the best leverage.
3. Hide a treat under the water bottle, box or just behind the door.
4. The dog will naturally put his nose to the bottom of the bottle, box or door to sniff the treat.
5. Cue, "Push."
6. When the dog pushes hard enough to get the treat, reward.
7. Challenge 3 other Players to a push race.
8. Create a start and finish line.
9. At the same time have the dogs push their own weighted box over the finish line.

Create a variation of this game here:

Put

Intermediate, Advanced

Purpose: challenge, to put an object on a table or chair, put (drop) trash in a container

What you will need: a toy or item the dog likes to hold, bathroom trash can or a medium-sized box

Instructions:

1. Use positive reinforcement.
2. Dog must know "Drop".
3. Use a container like a medium-sized box.
4. Have the dog pick up a designated item.
5. Put the box under the dog's chin and cue "Put/Drop".
6. Treat the drop.
7. Graduate to leaving the box on the floor for the "Put/Drop".
8. Graduate to having the dog "Put/Drop" on a chair.
9. Extinguish the "Drop".
10. Graduate to "Put" on a table.
11. Challenge other Players to have their dog put a toy on a chair, on a table and in a box. Increase the difficulty. The winner is the dog that accomplishes all on the first try.

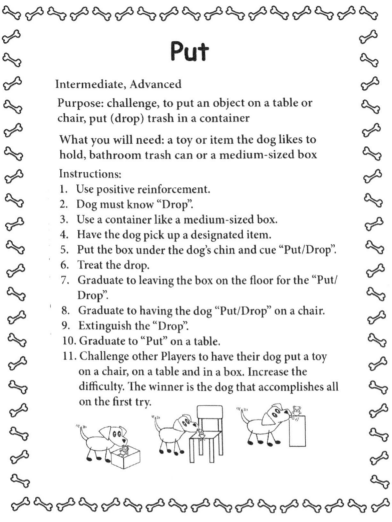

Create a variation of this game here:

Read the Cue Card

Intermediate, Advanced

Purpose: cue exercise, item discrimination

What you will need: 5 large cards with cues printed on them

Instructions:
1. Use positive reinforcement.
2. Make the large, cue cards that are shown below.
3. Put your hands on the cards as they are shown below. For instance, hold the cue card "Sit" on the top of the card. Then say, "Sit."
4. Make one card proficient at a time.
5. Extinguish the verbal cue. The card and where you put your hands become the cue. It is a different form of a hand signal.

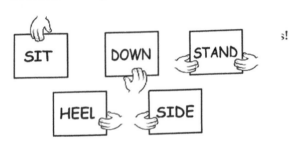

Create a variation of this game here:

Red Light/Green Light

All levels

Purpose: cue exercise

What you will need: rewards

Instructions:
1. Use positive reinforcement.
2. One Player will be a caller.
3. Everyone else will handle a dog.
4. All Players with dogs will be at one end of the room.
5. The caller will be at the other end of the room.
6. A positional cue will be called by the caller such as "Sit".
7. When the caller says, "Green light", the row of Players with dogs move forward.
8. When the caller says, "Red Light", the dogs and Players stop and the dogs are cued to "Sit".
9. The caller will mix up the "Green light" and "Red light" to fool the Players.
10. If a dog team moves on the "Red light" then that team is out of the game.

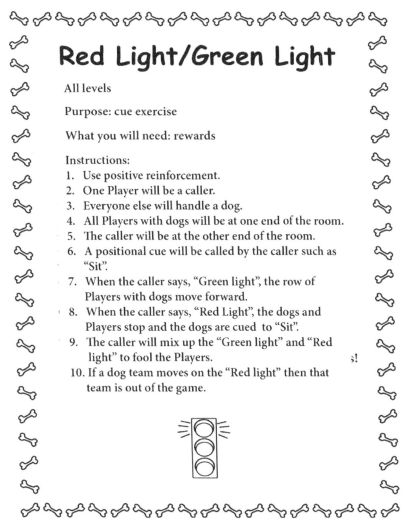

Create a variation of this game here:

Relay Race
Assortment

Advanced

Purpose: challenge, cue exercise

What you will need: touch lights, buckets to put a toy in, large boxes to push

Instructions:
1. Dog to be solid in "Push", "Put" and "Touch".
2. Set up 2 or more teams.
3. Each team will have the dog "Push" a box, then "Put" a toy in a bucket, then "Touch" a touch light, then run back to the start and tag the next Player and dog.

Create a variation of this game here:

Relay Race
Bring

All levels

Purpose: challenge, self-control

What you will need: pile of retrieval items

Instructions:
1. Dogs to have retrieval skills.
2. Make a large pile of different, fun retrieval items.
3. Create 2 or more teams, 2 or more per team.
4. On the "Go" the first member of each team sends their dog to retrieve any item from the pile and return it to the person.
5. Then the next team member sends their dog out to retrieve from the pile and return with the item. And so on.

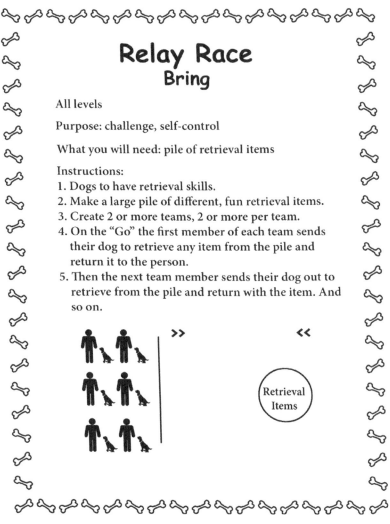

Create a variation of this game here:

Relay Race
Positions

All levels

Purpose: cue exercise

What you will need: cones or mats

Instructions:
1. Set rows of cones, 4 cones per row, 4 feet apart.
2. Line up teams at the start of each row.
3. Assign each cone/mat in the row a position (see below).
4. Teams to race each other up and back with the dog displaying the assigned cues at each cone.
5. Handler taps the next team member to go.

		>>			<<	
	Sit	Down	Stand	Front		
	Sit	Down	Stand	Front		
	Sit	Down	Stand	Front		

Create a variation of this game here:

Relay Race
Push Pull

Advanced

Purpose: cue exercise

What you will need: 3 things on wheels with rope attached, large heavy boxes or something similar, yellow tape

Instructions:
1. Create 2 or more teams with 2 dogs in each team.
2. Place the push items about 10-12 feet from the pull item.
3. Put yellow tape on the floor as the line for the dog to push (Page 73) the box over and to the pull (Pagen107) to an item over.
4. On the "Go" the first team in line takes their dog to push the box over the yellow line, then pull the wheeled item over the yellow line.
5. Run back to the start and send off the next team member.

Create a variation of this game here:

Relay Race
Put

Advanced

Purpose: challenge

What you will need: items for 3 teams (6 beanbags or small toys, 12 plastic buckets)

Instructions:
1. Dogs to be skilled in retrieval and "Put". (Page 74)
2. Create 3 teams with 2 or more Players with dogs on each team.
3. Set 4 buckets in a line for each team.
4. Put a beanbag or small toy into the 1st and 3rd buckets for each team.
5. On the "Go" the first Players in line run to the first bucket. The dog is cued to get the beanbag, carry it to the 2nd bucket and drop it in.
6. Then they run to the 3rd bucket, get the beanbag and drop it in the 4th bucket.
7. The Players run back to the start and tag the next runners.

Create a variation of this game here:

Roll the Dice

All levels

Purpose: cue exercise

What you will need: sets of dice

Instructions:
1. Hand each Player a dice.
2. Each Player to put their dog into a "Down/Stay".
3. First Player tosses a dice and must demonstrate as many cues as the dots on the dice.
4. Every Player takes a turn.

Create a variation of this game here:

Same

Intermediate, Advanced

Purpose: challenge

What you will need: treats, 5 items that are the same such as five white socks or 5 flip flops

Instructions:

1. Use positive reinforcement.
2. Dog to have retrieval skills.
3. Create one or more secure areas. (Rooms or X-pens depending on how many dogs are playing)
4. In the secure area(s) place a box, a chair, a small rug and other things that one of the "Same" items can be placed.
5. Have another Player take <u>4</u> of the 5 "Same" items and place them randomly around the secure area on, under and in things.
6. The Player with the dog will hold the 5th item.
7. Go into the secure area and have the dog "Sit" and face you. Show the dog the 5th item and cue "Same".
8. Encourage the dog to search around the area.
9. When the dog finds a "Same" item, cue the dog to "Get it" and bring it to you.
10. Increase difficulty as the dog gets better.

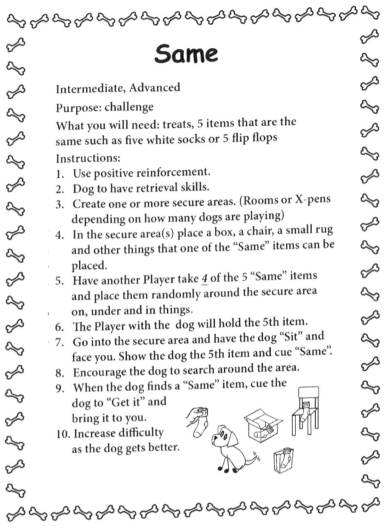

Create a variation of this game here:

Same
Balls in a Pool

Advanced

Purpose: challenge, retrieve a matching item in a high distraction environment

What you will need: baby plastic pool, multi-colored child's plastic fun balls, duplicate retrieval items

Instructions:
1. Use positive reinforcement.
2. Start by placing a toy in the pool, on the balls.
3. Hold a duplicate in your hand behind your back.
4. Have the dog sit and look at you.
5. Show the dog the item you have behind your back and cue, "Same/Get it."
6. The dog must retrieve the same item you are holding from the ball pool.
7. Increase the difficulty by using different pairs of things.
8. Put random items in the pool that the dog has to ignore while searching for a same item to retrieve.

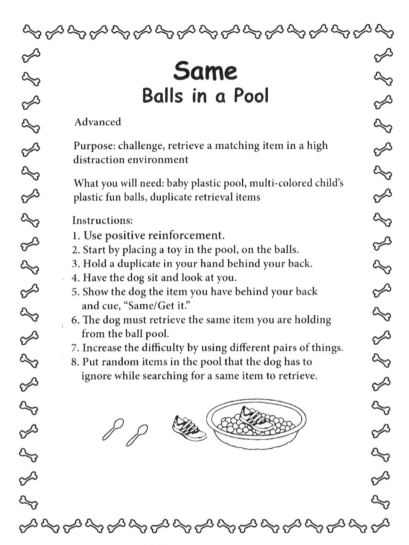

Create a variation of this game here:

Same
Pile

Intermediate, Advanced

Purpose: challenge

What you will need: treats and clicker, 2 sets of 5 items that are the same such as five white socks and 5 plastic water bottles

Instructions:
1. Use positive reinforcement.
2. Create 2 teams.
3. Pile the same items about 5 feet from the teams.
4. One Player trainer takes a sock.
5. The other Player takes a bottle.
6. The Player with the sock puts their dog into a "Sit"and shows the dog the sock.
7. The Player cues "Same" and points to the pile of stuff.
8. When the dog finds a "Same" item (sock), cue the dog to "Get it" and bring it to you.
9. If the dog brings the bottle instead, take it, and thank the dog and put the item back into the pile.
10. Send the dog back to the pile to try again.
11. Repeat with the bottles.
12. Keep the game going until all the items are retrieved.

Create a variation of this game here:

Sawhorses

All levels

Purpose: challenge, body awareness

What you will need: sawhorses of different heights

Instructions:
1. Use the saw horses to teach the following: "Over", "Under" and "Through".
2. Mix it up. Have the dogs jump all of the sawhorses or go through all of them, etc.
3. Set up a second set of sawhorses so 2 dogs can compete.

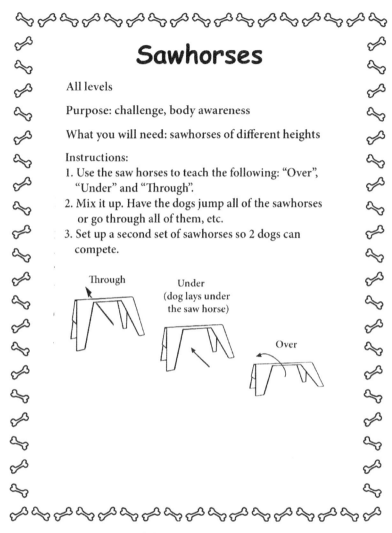

Through

Under
(dog lays under
the saw horse)

Over

Create a variation of this game here:

Shell Game

Beginner

Purpose: challenge, problem-solving

What you will need: treats, small toy, 3 cups or 3 small bowls

Instructions:
1. Use positive reinforcement.
2. Have the dog "Sit" in front of three cups or 3 bowls.
3. Put a treat under a cup or bowl.
4. Shuffle the cups or bowls around so it is not obvious where you put the treat.
5. Cue the dog to "Get it".
6. Let the dog find the treat.
7. Now put a small toy under a cup or bowl.

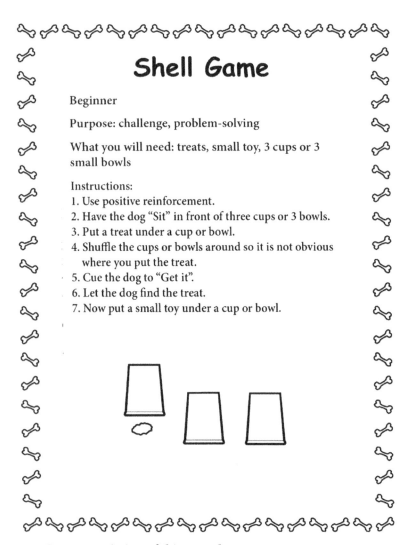

Create a variation of this game here:

Simon Says

Beginner

Purpose: cue exercise

What you will need: dogs

Instructions:
1. 3 or more Players with dogs.
2. One Player is Simon.
3. Simon issues cues by saying, for example, "Simon, says, "Have your dog's sit."
4. The Players should only comply if the phrase starts with "Simon, says".
5. Players are eliminated from the game by either following instructions that do not have "Simon says", or by failing to follow an instruction.

Create a variation of this game here:

Sleeping Dogs

All levels

Purpose: cue exercise

What you will need: rewards

Instructions:
1. Use positive reinforcement.
2. One Player plays the Hunter.
3. All dogs to be in a "Down/Stay".
4. The Hunter goes around to each dog and tries to break their stay by annoying them without saying the dog's name, touching them or scaring them.
5. Put a 2nd Hunter into the game.
6. The dog that breaks the "Stay" is out.
7. Change the dog's position to a "Sit/Stay" and a "Down/Stay".

Create a variation of this game here:

Sniff

Beginner

Purpose: recall, reward, to allow dog to relax

What you will need: treats and clicker

Instructions:
1. Use positive reinforcement.
2. Use the cue, "Sniff".
3. Encourage the dog to sniff a bush, pole or something other dogs might have peed on.
4. The sniffing is a treat all by itself.
5. Let the dog enjoy itself for 30-60 seconds then do a recall. Reward. Repeat many times.
6. Now have a group of Players invite their dogs to sniff something rich with doggie odor.
7. The first dog that recalls off the odor wins.

Create a variation of this game here:

Speak/Quiet

All levels

Purpose: cue exercise, to teach dog to alert bark

What you will need: an item the dog desperately wants and may bark to get it

Instructions:

1. Use positive reinforcement.
2. Get the dog excited by a special toy or a knock on the door.
3. When the dog barks cue, "Speak." Reward.
4. If the dog will not bark from excitement in a setup then you will have to capture it when someone knocks on the door or at another time when the dog may bark.
5. Use hands signals to "Speak" and "Quiet". (Hand signals, Pages 36 & 37)
6. Once the dog learns to bark on cue, the bark becomes a reward by itself. Then you reward only on the quiet.
7. Challenge other Players to have their dogs "Speak" 3 times, then 4 times and so on.
8. The dog that speaks out of turn is out of the game.
9. The dog that barks the most in a row wins!

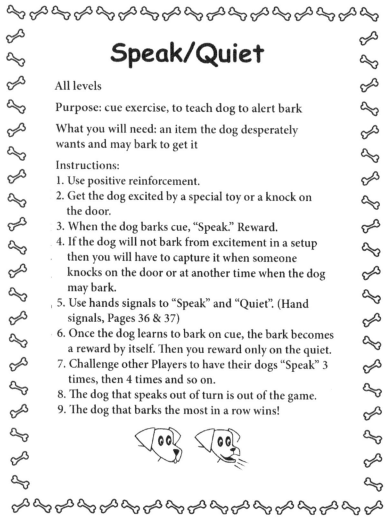

Create a variation of this game here:

Spin

Beginner

Purpose: body awareness, fun, position refinement

What you will need: treats

Instructions:
1. Use positive reinforcement.
2. With a treat held close to the dog's nose lure the dog into a spin clockwise then counter clockwise.
3. You will be able to tell which direction the dog most easily spins. A few dogs can go either way.
4. Once the direction is determined then cue "Spin" (Hand signal, Page 37) and lure the dog into a tight spin.
5. Click-treat at the end of the spin.
6. Extinguish the lure.

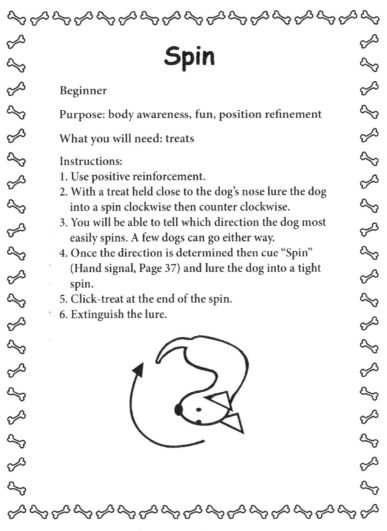

Create a variation of this game here:

Spin the Bottle

All levels

Purpose: cue exercise

What you will need: a full water bottle to spin

Instructions:
1. Have all Players with their dogs form a circle.
2. Put the water bottle in the middle of the circle.
3. The person with the oldest dog goes first.
4. That person spins the bottle.
5. The bottle stops and the cap points at someone.
6. The spinner of the bottle tells that person to do
   3 puppy push-ups. (Page 72)
7. Then the puppy push-up Player becomes the
   next spinner and so on.
8. Add difficulty by having the dog perform more
   difficult behaviors.

Create a variation of this game here:

Stairs

All levels

Purpose: body awareness, cue exercise, handler trust

What you will need: stairs

Instructions:
1. Same as Puppy Push-ups but on stairs. (Page 72)
2. Add "Move up", "Back", "About face", "Forward", "Follow" and walking backwards on the stairs.
3. Players cue their dogs 3 behaviors on the stairs in the first round.
4. In the second round Players repeat their first string of cues and add one more cue, now 4.
5. In the third round Players even add one more cue, now 5. And so on.
6. When a Player's dog doesn't do the cue asked that team is out.
7. Last team standing, wins!

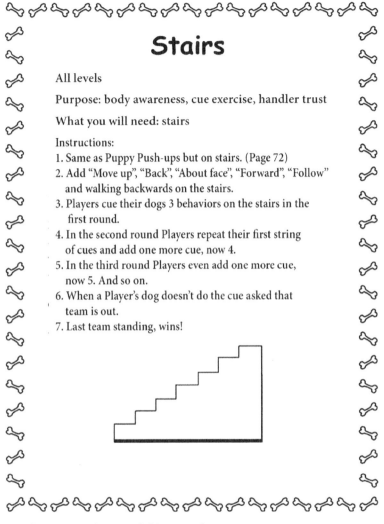

Create a variation of this game here:

Steady

Beginner

Purpose: body awareness, calming, self-control

What you will need: rewards

Instructions:
1. Use positive reinforcement.
2. Have the dog "Sit", "Down", or "Stand" in front of you.
3. Normally the dog's tail will be moving.
4. Cue, "Steady." When the tail stops moving, reward.
5. The more you train "Steady" the faster the dog's body goes calm when you need it.
6. Have all Players "Steady" their dogs at the same time.
7. The dog that steadies first wins!

Create a variation of this game here:

Stuck

All levels

Purpose: challenge, problem-solving

What you will need: long stick the dog likes

Instructions:
1. Find a long stick that dog is jazzed over.
2. Have the dog with the stick on one side of the door and you on the other side.
3. Cue the dog to get the stick.
4. Let the dog figure out how to get it through the door to you.

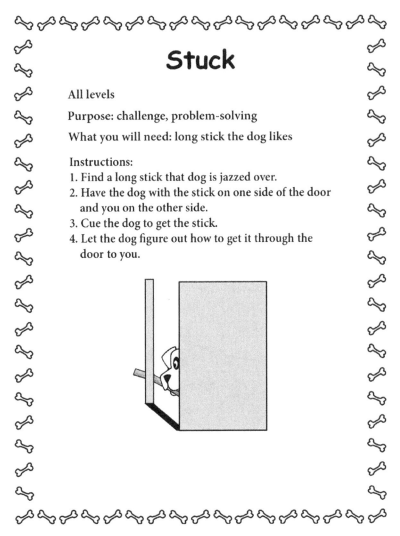

Create a variation of this game here:

Tennis Ball Muffins

Beginner

Purpose: persistence, retrieval

What you will need: 6 hole, muffin tin and a 12 hole, muffin tin; enough tennis balls to fill tins

Instructions:
1. Start with the 6 hole muffin tin.
2. Put a tennis ball in each hole.
3. Without the dog watching you, put a treat under one tennis ball.
4. Cue the dog to "Get it" (meaning to find the treat that is under one of the balls).
5. Graduate to the larger tin.

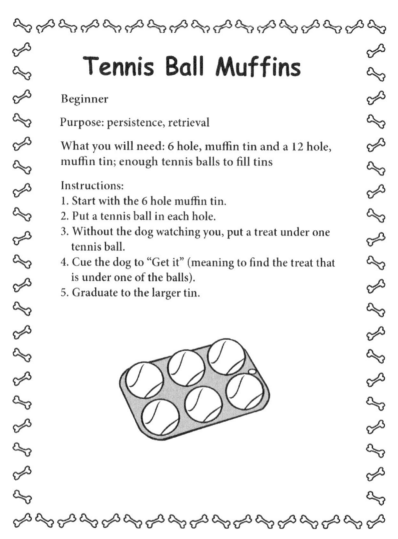

Create a variation of this game here:

The Wave

Beginner

Purpose: cue exercise

What you will need: rewards

Instructions:
1. This is like a wave at the stadium but doggie style.
2. Two teams. Five people with their dogs on each team.
3. Set up two rows of 5 chairs facing each other.
4. Leave enough room between each chair so the dogs will sit easily at a heel.
5. On a "Go" from one of the players, the people at the beginning of each row will stand and cue their dog to "Stand" at the same time.
6. Then the next person repeats.
7. When the row finishes, the person at the end of the row starts again by sitting in the chair at the same time the person tells their dog to "Sit".
8. The row that finishes their wave first, wins!

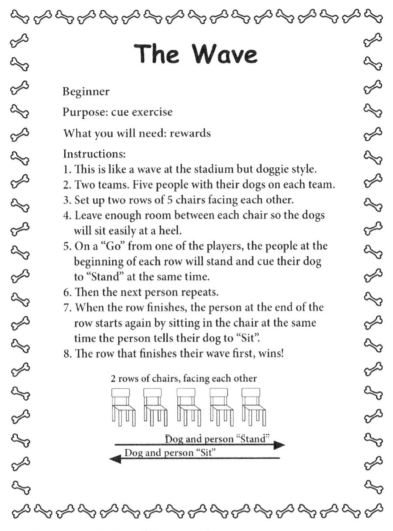

2 rows of chairs, facing each other

Dog and person "Stand" ▶

◀ Dog and person "Sit"

Create a variation of this game here:

Tic-Tac-Toe
Positions

Intermediate, Advanced

Purpose: self-control, stays

What you will need: 9 small rugs or vinyl tiles, 6 blue bandannas and 6 red bandannas

Instructions:
1. Put the bandannas on 12 dogs to make 2 teams.
2. Flip a coin to see which team goes first.
3. The team that wins the toss chooses what position the dogs will stay in for the game. (Sit, Down or Stand)
4. If a dog doesn't hold the stay, the dog leaves the game and the opposing team gets to go again.
5. When one team gets three dogs in a row that team wins.

Create a variation of this game here:

Tic Tac Toe
Put

Advanced

Purpose: cue exercise, self-control, "Put" (Page 74)

What you will need: 9 buckets, 9 items to drop into the buckets, 6 blue bandannas & 6 red bandannas

Instructions:
1. Put the bandannas on 12 dogs to make 2 teams.
2. Flip a coin to see which team goes first.
3. The team that wins the toss chooses what position the dogs will stay in for the game.
4. Each dog to "Put" an item into a bucket to claim that spot.
5. The dog has 3 tries to get the item into the bucket.
6. If the dog misses 3 times then that team loses its turn.
7. The team that gets three buckets in a row wins.

Create a variation of this game here:

Tires

Beginner

Purpose: body awareness

What you will need: 5 to 8 used tires

Instructions:
1. Line up the tires flat on the floor against a wall.
2. With the dog on leash encourage the dog to walk over the tires.

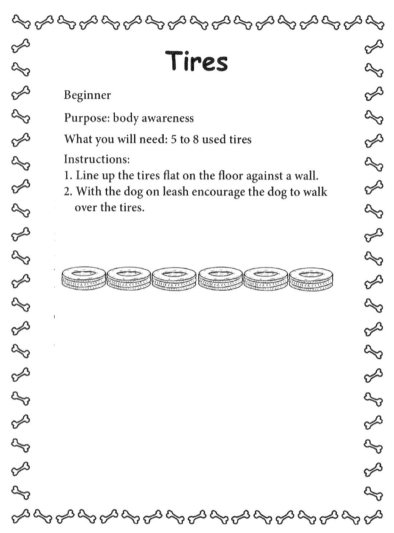

Create a variation of this game here:

Tires
Retrieve

Intermediate, Advanced

Purpose: body awareness, challenge, retrieval

What you will need: 5 to 8 tires, retrieval items

Instructions:
1. Line up the tires flat on the floor against a wall.
2. With the dog on leash encourage the dog to walk over the tires.
3. Put an item to retrieve at the end of the row of tires.
4. Have the dog retrieve the item then "Put" (Page 74) the item in another tire for the next dog.
5. Repeat with others dogs.
6. Increase the difficulty of the retrieval items and repeat the exercise.
7. The winner is the dog that retrieved all the difficult items.

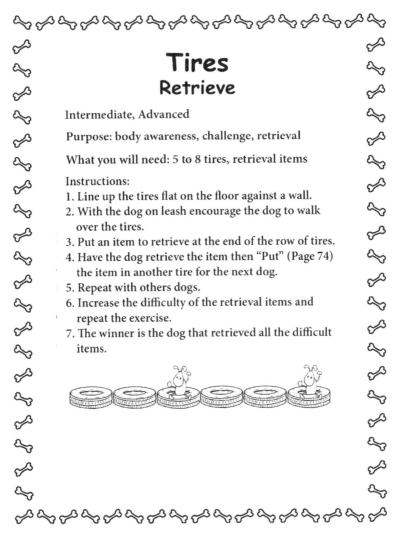

Create a variation of this game here:

Towel
Tug

Intermediate, Advanced

Purpose: retrieval

What you will need: towel on a rack; skilled tug (Page 107)

Instructions:
1. Use positive reinforcement.
2. Hold the edge of the towel while on the rack and cue the dog to "Towel/Tug".
3. Once the dog learns to pull the towel completely off the rack extinguish the "Tug".
4. Have the dog put the towel in your hand.

Create a variation of this game here:

Toy Under Bed

All levels

Purpose: challenge, problem-solving, retrieval

What you will need: dog's favorite toy

Instructions:
1. Use positive reinforcement.
2. Put the toy next to the bed for the dog to retrieve.
3. Then put the item partly under the bed for retrieval.
4. Then put the item a few inches under the bed for retrieval.
5. Then put the toy deeper under the bed so the dog has to think how to get it.
6. Have the dog use "Paw" to get the item. (Page 62)
7. Try this game with different retrieval items.

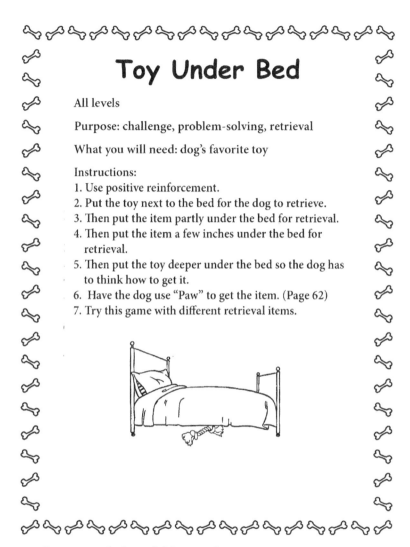

Create a variation of this game here:

Treat the Trainer

Beginner

Purpose: rewarding the trainer for doing it right

What you will need: M & Ms

Instructions:
1. One Player has a cup of M & Ms.
2. The Player with the candy watches the other Players train.
3. Players that
   ~ are consistent
   ~ use the dog's name before a cue
   ~ say the cue once
   ~ follow through
   ~ have a loose leash
   are rewarded with a candy.

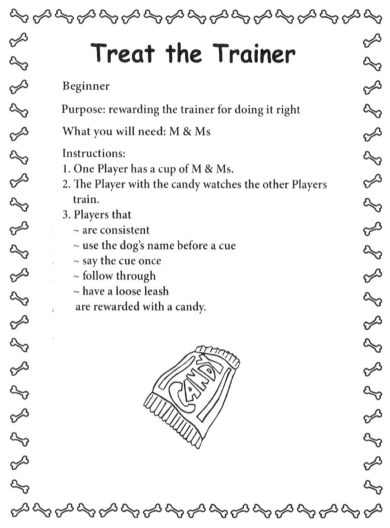

Create a variation of this game here:

Tree Retrieve

All levels

Purpose: problem-solving, retrieval

What you will need: retrieval items

Instructions:
1. Use positive reinforcement.
2. Put the dog's favorite retrieval item in a low crook in a tree.
3. As the dog succeeds put it higher in the tree but still reachable.
4. Try different items.

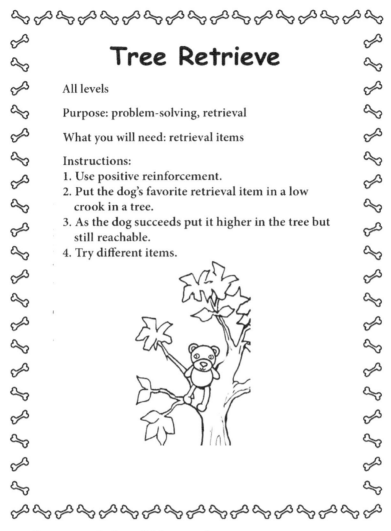

Create a variation of this game here:

Tug of War

All levels

Purpose: reward, self control; used for opening doors getting a towel off a rack, pulling a zipper, etc. (Pages 103, 114)

What you will need: rope or other appropriate items to tug on

Instructions:
1. Use positive reinforcement.
2. The key is to have the dog "Tug" an item with an even, pull strength and to "Drop" the item on cue. No jerking or uneven tugs. A controlled tug.
3. Jiggle the tug item in front of the dog. Let him grab it.
4. Lean back on the pull so the pull is even.
5. Cue the dog to "Drop" by dropping a treat on the floor or trading the tug item for a treat or another toy.

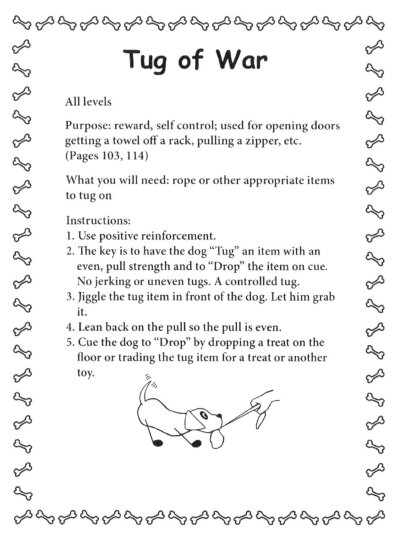

Create a variation of this game here:

Tunnel

All levels

Purpose: body awareness, confidence, getting used to an enclosed space

What you will need: agility tunnel, retrieval items, crate

Instructions:
1. Start by letting the dog run through the stand-alone tunnel.
2. Add the tunnel to your maze or attach it to a crate so the dog has to run through the tunnel into a crate, retrieve an item and return through the tunnel.
3. Be creative.

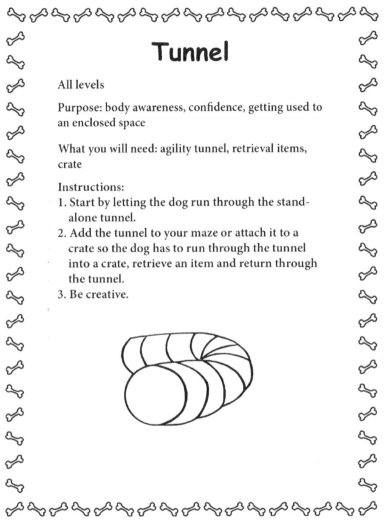

Create a variation of this game here:

Up, Up-Up

Advanced

Purpose: advanced retrieve, challenge, to teach dog to retrieve an item from a high shelf

What you will need: retrieval items, layered shelving

Instructions:
1. Use positive reinforcement.
2. Dog must have a solid retrieve.
3. Find a bookcase or anything stable with two levels that a dog can go up on.
4. Lure the dog to go "Up" on the first shelf. Cue,"Up."
5. Then lure the dog to the next higher shelf. Cue, "Up-up."
6. Add retrieval items.

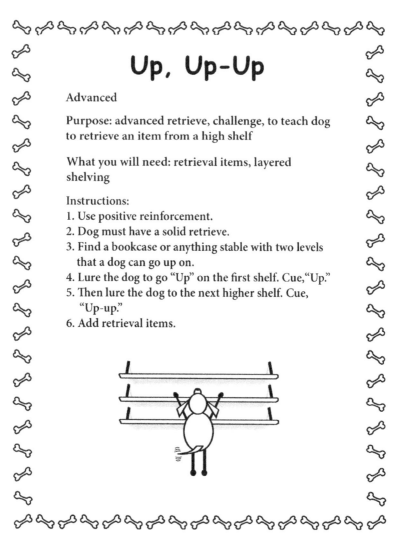

Create a variation of this game here:

Wave

Beginner

Purpose: greeting

What you will need: rewards

Instructions:
1. Use positive reinforcement.
2. Dog needs a solid "Shake".
3. Cue the dog to "Wave-Shake".
4. When the dog puts its paw up to "Shake" pull your hand away, then put your hand back as though to shake again.
5. Repeat 3 times.
6. The dog will appear to wave.
7. Extinguish the "Shake".

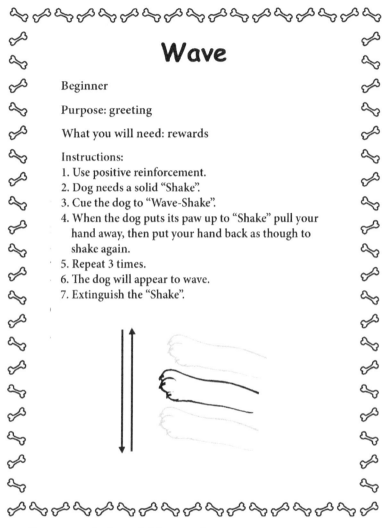

Create a variation of this game here:

What?

Beginner

Purpose: to get the dog to tilt its head on cue

What you will need: rewards

Instructions:
1. Use positive reinforcement.
2. Put the dog in a "Sit/Stay" or "Down/Stay".
3. Cue, "What?"
4. Then make a high pitched sound with your voice.
5. When the dog tilts its head in response to the sound reward.
6. Do this training on the fly (off and on during the week). The high pitched sound needs to surprise the dog.
7. Over time drop the sound.

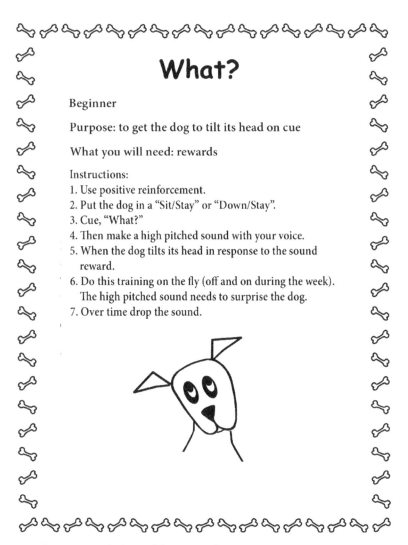

Create a variation of this game here:

Whisper Cues

Beginner

Purpose: cue exercise, eye contact between person and dog

What you will need: dogs

Instructions:
1. Use positive reinforcement.
2. Whisper a string of cues to the dog.
3. Compete by seeing which dog does the most whisper cues in a row.

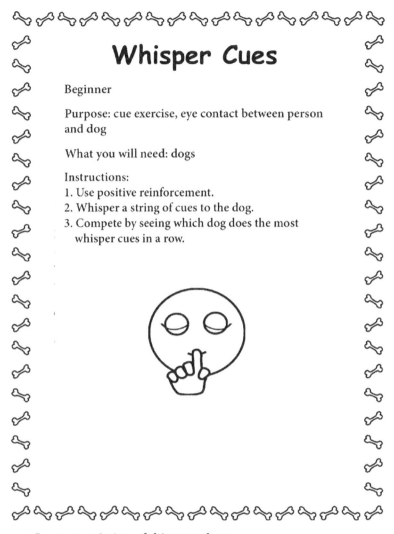

Create a variation of this game here:

Yellow Ball

Intermediate, Advanced

Purpose: challenge, item discrimination, retrieval, self-control

What you will need: yellow balls, red balls, blue balls

Instructions:

1. Use positive reinforcement.
2. The dog already has retrieval skills.
3. Put the dog in a "Sit/Stay".
4. Put the yellow ball a few feet in front of the dog.
5. Cue, "Yellow/Get it".
6. When the dog brings the yellow ball to you, reward.
7. Repeat many times around the room.
8. Then put down 5 yellow balls near each other. Repeat 3-7.
9. Add one blue ball with the group of yellow balls. Repeat #5-#7.
10. If the dog retrieves the blue ball instead of the yellow, thank him, then send him out to get a yellow for the reward.
11. Now add a red ball to the one blue ball and yellow balls on the floor. Repeat the above.
12. Now repeat the exercise with red and blue balls with one yellow ball in the mix.

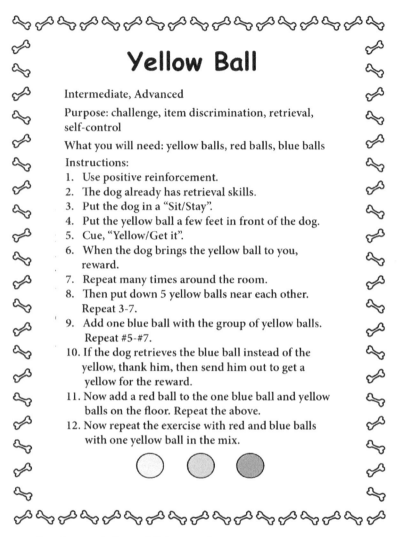

Create a variation of this game here:

Zipper Purse
Tug

Intermediate, Advanced

Purpose: challenge, cue exercise, teach the dog to pull a zipper

What you will need: small zipper purse with treats inside

Instructions:
1. Use positive reinforcement.
2. Teach "Tug" first. (Page 107)
3. Show the dog the end of pull tab.
4. Every time he touches it, reward.
5. Then encourage the dog to "Get it", "Tug".
6. Reward for even the slightest tug.
7. When the dog gives a solid tug where the zipper moves, reward by giving the treat from the purse.
8. Progress until the dog unzips the purse all the way.

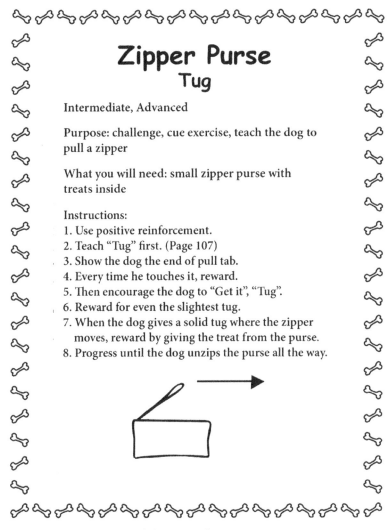

Create a variation of this game here:

31270181R00076

Made in the USA
Middletown, DE
29 December 2018